D0890561

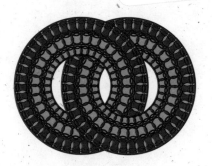

JESUS WAS A HOMEBOY

KEVIN CAREY

ALSO BY KEVIN CAREY

The Beach People (2014)
The One Fifteen to Penn Station (2012)

JESUS

WAS   A

HOMEBOY

KEVIN CAREY

CavanKerry ◈ Press LTD.

Copyright © 2016 by Kevin Carey

All rights reserved. No part of this book may be used, reproduced, or adapted to public performances in any manner whatsoever without permission from the publisher, except in the case of brief quotations embodied in critical articles and reviews. For more information, write to Permissions, CavanKerry Press, 6 Horizon Road, Fort Lee, New Jersey 07024.

CavanKerry Press Ltd.
Fort Lee, New Jersey
www.cavankerrypress.org

Publisher's Cataloging-in-Publication
(*Provided by Quality Books, Inc.*)

    Carey, Kevin, 1957- author.
      [Poems. Selections]
      Jesus was a homeboy / Kevin Carey. —First edition.
      pages cm
      ISBN 978-1-933880-55-6

      1. Autobiographical poetry.   I. Title.

    PS3603.A7416A6 2016   811'.6
                QBI16-1117

Cover photograph by Suzy Blase
Cover and interior text design by Ryan Scheife, Mayfly Design
First Edition 2016, Printed in the United States of America

EMERGING VOICES
CavanKerry ® Press

CavanKerry Press is dedicated to springboarding the careers of previously unpublished, early, and mid-career poets by bringing to print two to three Emerging Voices annually. Manuscripts are selected from open submission; Cavankerry Press does not conduct competitions.

CavanKerry Press is grateful for the support it receives from the New Jersey State Council on the Arts.

for my mom

Have I seen an angel? Oh, have I seen a ghost?
Where's that rock of ages? When I need it most?

—Johnny Cash

CONTENTS

I

Summer Storms   3

The Weird Kid   5

Sarasota Airport, 1984   6

Creative Writing at Osgood Park, Salem, September 7, 2010   7

Newburyport   9

Another Coffee Shop   11

Navajo Salesman   12

Reincarnation   13

A Holiday Poem   14

A Surreal Poem   15

Delayed   16

Chicago   17

The Center   19

Before the Devil Knows You're Dead   20

II

The Home Movie   23

Fairy Tale   24

My Father's Son   25

Always   26

Justice   28

Getting It Right   30

Revere Beach after Hours   31

Looking at an Old Man in the Pleasant Street Tea Room   32

Five Days of Rain Dreams   34

Witness   35

Jesus Was a Homeboy   36

Wishing Well   37

Not Much to It   39

III

Things I've Lost   43

From Another Day   44

Poetry Snob   45

The Same Old Story   46

Siberian Dwarfs   47

Bob's Story   48

Get Thee to a Nunnery   49

At the Car Hop, 2015   50

Coffee Shop   51

Motion Picture Family   52

Heaven   55

Death Wish   56

Waiting   57

Reading to My Kids   58

Acknowledgments   61

JESUS WAS A HOMEBOY

KEVIN CAREY

Summer Storms

They haunt me,
these people.
They creep in after a song
or a conversation I overhear.
They hide in the walls
of my old bedroom,
stand in the shadows
of the schoolyard,
one with a brain tumor,
one crossing the street to get
a cheeseburger, one with a gun
in the basement of his house.
I think of them today,
watching the rain outside,
heavy drops of summer
pounding the pavement
washing away the heat,
some of the memories I can't face.
The sky flashes and I think,
When did the lightning start to scare me?
As a kid I loved the summer storms,
hunkered in my room by my closet,
the walls of my mother's house
much stronger than my own.
There are days now when everything
frightens me, my own impending death,
the quick dark skies
and their wild bursts of light,
the violence in everyone waiting to erupt,
the randomness,
the wrong step on the wrong highway,
the wrong movie theater on the wrong night,

the empty street in a lightning storm,
where a young kid stands
under the open sky expecting
his mother's arms to hold him,
going dark, never knowing what hit him.

The Weird Kid

I was the weird kid in grammar school.
I was shy, I made noises when I walked,
strange gulping sounds in my throat,
and I stuttered when we read out loud.
But I was not without talent. I could roll
my stomach like a belly dancer
(a big hit in the coatroom closet),
I used to do it while singing "My Baby Does
the Hanky Panky," and I could make myself
turn red by holding my breath.
On good days I got closer to a deep purple.
Sharon Malfitano, the class president,
sat behind me. She had an election poster
of Dracula saying, "All I vant is your vote."
Sometimes during a test or when we were drawing,
I would turn around and stop breathing
and tighten the muscles in my neck
and quickly my white Irish skin would turn
the shade of a radish and she'd smile
and eventually if I held it long enough
she's start laughing at me. I guess you could say
I had a way with the ladies.

Sarasota Airport, 1984

They're in Florida for the season
but I decide I need to see them,
make it right between us.
So I step off the plane from Boston
and wait at the terminal at Sarasota
for them to pick me up.
I had four drinks at Logan
and two more on the plane.
I'm dressed in jeans, cowboy boots,
and a button-down white shirt.
I'm wearing big round aviators,
smoking a cigarette, and waiting outside
with a duffle bag of clothes, the air heavy
and humid. I see pelicans
flying over the runway,
palm trees along the horizon
and I suddenly feel light-headed,
maybe from the heat, maybe
from the early day's drinks
or the drinks the night before.
I see my father pulling in,
my mother in the passenger seat
and I remember the phone call,
telling them I'd like to come visit,
the silence on the other end.
They pull up in front of me
and I hold the cloth strap of my bag
heavy in my hand and whisper to myself,
This was not a good idea.

Creative Writing at Osgood Park, Salem, September 7, 2010

He knows we are the enemy.
We're from the college up the street.
It's a private park, his park.
He pays dues.
You wouldn't understand,
he thinks. *Once they start coming…*
He is afraid.
He knows things about poets,
(the seeds they may be planting).
They'll never stop, he says.
Already they are scribbling in
black-bound journals,
small spiral notebooks,
some on scraps of torn paper.
He spots one or two creeping
over the green trimmed lawn
like ants, he thinks.
He turns and points, *More of them, look!*
He is right. They are inching across
the sea-swollen pier, soon to be slipping
beneath the roped-off blue water,
hiding in the mud on the ocean floor,
to always be there and never leave.
He stomps his feet on the ground.
He knows they have spread too far,
slithering between the white fence pickets
around the patio fieldstones,
past the clean swept and weeded driveways.
Never, never leave, he shouts.
They are burrowing in the sand,
darkening the sky like locusts,
hanging from the limbs of trees,

rocking the wind-driven waves
with their words,
Nooooo! he screams.
They are filling the air
with a deafening hum,
they are fighting,
they are sacrificing,
they are marching,
they are banging on his dead-bolted door,
they are chanting,
we are here
we are here
we are here.

Newburyport

Last week, packing our things to move
back to the North Shore after renting
near Boston for a year, my daughter
and I argued outside the rented house.
She's already leaving me.
I will miss the coffee shop on Dorchester Ave.,
the quick ride into the city,
the track at Milton Academy.
I'm still mourning the Celtics' loss
to the Heat in seven games.
Now, as I fly home from Chicago
after moving my son into his apartment
(we carried furniture in 100 degrees,
and today we hugged after breakfast on
North Michigan Avenue), I'm reminded
of a friend who found out
he is going to lose his colon,
and it's about all I can take, the sadness
like a wave of heat in front of me,
and I wish summer would hurry up
and get over so I can start new
while all the leaves are dying around me,
forget that these moments are racing past,
grab a goodbye from the air
and hold it, maybe let it pull me back
to a simpler time when I was too busy
to wonder as much, too tired to think,
when I'd drive my kids to the playground
in Newburyport, the thick gray blocks
piled twelve feet high, watch them
climb like squirrels in and out

of the open spaces, up and down the slide.
It was all I needed then, a cool fall day,
my kids climbing something, my back
against a wooden bench watching,
a cup of tea warming my hands.

Another Coffee Shop

My friend tells me
some bad news about his kid
and I can't get it out of my mind.
I think of it in the morning
when I sit in a new coffee shop,
the way I used to sit in a new barroom,
watching the downtown traffic
and waiting for something to change.

I feel the hurt in my friend's heart
as if it were my own,
and I selfishly wonder if things will be different
with us now, the jokes,
the irreverent conversation,
the easy way we tell each other everything.
Nothing ever stays the same, does it?
Some disruption is always lurking,
like the first crack of thunder.

I write my stories in my new corner,
sip tea, and wait for the phone to ring,
look up now and then
at the gray winter haze holding back the sun.

Navajo Salesman

Somewhere before Taos, I see the czar
of six-inch kachinas with a belt buckle
as big as Santa Fe. *Boston,* he says.
I have to get there. The dry wind billows
the turquoise cloth around us, shades us
from the desert sun. *Not bad,* I tell him,
thumbing an arrowhead made of colored quartz.
Handmade, he smiles. *Fifteen dollars.*

Back home I know the street vendors, too,
the way they work the tourists, every day
the same sell, setting up and breaking down,
opening and closing boxes of photographs,
baseball caps, T-shirts. I put the arrowhead
back in its place alongside some beaded chokers
and a sandstone etching of an Indian headdress.
The beads are two for ten, he tells me.

Outside I look to the desert running
for miles away from me, the wired waves
of heat across the Navajo reservation,
and it seems like all reservations to me,
bleak and barren and void of vegetation.
I tuck my hands in my pockets
my fingers resting on the dollar bills
still folded and waiting, the sun hot and
hanging in the cloudless sky,
the red-rock mountains rising in the distance
like something fake and forbidden.

Reincarnation

The Same Mistakes (Again)
Different Days

A Holiday Poem

It's Thanksgiving. I am drunk
at my sister-in-law's, my mother
and father looking at me sideways
in the chair. I tell a story I told
an hour ago, the one about Bill Burton
working the night shift,
saying to a customer, *We're here
to make friends, not money,*
and my father reminds me
it's the second time I've told it.
I slump in the chair, embarrassed
at the correction, and there is
a thick silence as we pass the turkey
and the stuffing. I am the drunk nephew,
the drunk brother, the drunk son,
and everyone can see me.
But I know my father sees his father,
reckless (and I would say more brave)
but liking the drink more than a person should.
He sees my future, maybe, long afternoons
in a Chelsea barroom, weekend benders,
a soggy liver, jaundice and dying in a sweat-soaked bed.
He hates what he sees, he's been through it already,
and once is more than enough.
Someone passes the pumpkin pie
and I think I hear him say, *No thanks, I'm full.*

A Surreal Poem

This is a surreal poem.
I'm not really sure what it means,
it's about my father
or a father figure or an aunt
with short hair,
or it's about love
or something like it
or maybe friendship or jealousy.
It's about what it's like to be
in high school from an older
perspective or through
the eyes of a child, cold
and waiting in an empty
schoolyard,
it's about Charles Simic
or about me at three a.m.
hung over or drunk or both
or neither,
it's about life or death
or like Johnny Cash might say
it's about *wounded angels shuffling
around the room* or maybe it's all
of these, or none of these, or
maybe it's about looking at a wave
crashing to the beach,
some sunny fall day,
a coiled fist of time
pounding the seconds off
the shore and I'm thinking,
This ain't so bad.

Delayed

I drink from a mug of tea and honey.
Outside, the fat raindrops
dance on the pavement,
people trot across the street
to their cars, midday headlights
moving east and west.
I see a text from my son
waiting at the airport in Chicago,
delayed. I see him in the long line
of holiday travelers, iPods and
cell phones.
The holidays are markers to me now.
We all come together to celebrate
the passing of another year—
the Hi-8 footage of my kids crawling
under a Christmas tree, both of
them standing on my thighs
at once like a circus family.
Now my shoulder hurts
just getting out of the car,
I'm a few days removed
from a weird virus,
and there's a humid winter rain outside.
Nothing is as it should be.
I should be a father
of young children forever,
little hands always holding mine,
wagons in tow, standing in deep dug
holes at the beach.
But time never listens.
It is stout and constant
and always doing what it pleases.

Chicago

South Dearborn Street,
tall black men,
buildings made of stone,
the garbage trucks grinding,
a circle of pigeons fans
over the rooftop of a restaurant—
open for breakfast.
The rumble of the Red Line
passing overhead,
my hand pressing on the glass,
reading the cold like Braille.
I am standing in my son's
apartment, a hazy sun,
everything gray and still
a city reflected in the lake.
He is in the North Loop
with his girlfriend.
Back home my wife and daughter
get ready to drive to D.C.
I stare out the window at
the picture of a city waking,
the pigeons circle again,
push further into the sky,
and I remember a time when
we were always together,
traveling in a pack,
to the store, to the Friendly's
at Gloucester Circle, to Ireland
and Spain, and it hits me
that I've been a fool to think
that time is my friend,
that there is plenty of it,

that it will be enough
if memory replaces this scene
in front of me like a postcard.
But I know the truth—
down the street, back East,
around the world—time is
leaking out of the pictures
like a hole in the dike.
If Dali were here, I would ask
him to stop his clocks from melting,
maybe catch the drippings
in a bucket, something we could
use later to recycle the minutes
that race past us like a bullet train.

The Center

for Bill Russell

You were always in the middle of it
your arms stretching from one side
of the lane to the other, tipping those
hopeless attempts just enough to gather
them and start the other way.

You touched everything, your fingertips
wrapped in white tape, your beard neat
to a point under your chin, your hands
on the shoulders of your teammates
during a time-out. You were the smartest man
they knew. The greatest Celtic.

Teams tried everything. Some were bigger,
some faster, some shooting better than you,
and all you ever did was win. I heard your name
at night from the radio on my bedside table,
the gravel voice of Johnny Most, *Russell* this,
Big Bill that. You were my hero.

Yet while you were winning eleven championships,
someone broke into your house
and defecated on your bed,
and sports guys said you were not happy,
you didn't sign autographs, you didn't
love Boston; how could you not?

I didn't know any of this then.
I only pounded the ball in my backyard
making layups as if I were you,
outstretched, driving to the basket,
beating them any way I could.

Before the Devil Knows You're Dead

Here's my wish: have them play some music,
something Irish, and sit me in a chair with my legs crossed,
an electric cigarette in my hand
so it looks like I'm on *The Dick Cavett Show.*
Have people come up randomly to say goodbye.
It's okay if they get into a shoving match,
knock down a floral arrangement or two,
and I want people to say something about me,
not sweet *I'll miss him* things but the truth—
he was a good guy most of the time,
he was funny, he was an asshole—
then I want them to put me on a wooden raft
with a poem, something I wrote that worked,
clip it to my chest and say, *Good luck,*
and set me off to sea, burning
like some Viking funeral pyre,
and turn around and have one on me,
for all the ones I had too early,
for all the ones I had to skip.

The Home Movie

It's 16-millimeter color footage of a pond in Concord,
my father, a white sailor's hat curled at the forehead,

shirtless, brown chest, an oar in each hand,
left then right, and me, six years old, sitting

across from him in the bow of the rowboat
as he works his way around the pond.

It was easier for him then. All he had to do
was look across to know I was safe,

no secrets, no worry, no phone calls at 3 a.m.
I can see it on his face, his whole life slowed down,

no future, no regrets, just the summer
for one long moment, the oars, my hand dipping

into the cool dark water around us,
the white birch trees sipping the shore,

the world and all its worry
miles and miles away from here.

Fairy Tale

for Betty

Is it true a woman in a clock shop
in Florida told you to go back to Boston
that day and I took the phone off the hook
because I was afraid to hear your voice?
Is it true that the person working behind me
said I was in trouble after you
walked up to the window on the beach
for the first time in forever and said, *Hi,*
a month before I made a big mistake?
Is it true that two years later we danced
on the top of the Parker House and drove
all over the West Coast of Ireland
listening to Frank Sinatra and Marshall Tucker,
and that both our kids were born
on rainy June mornings downtown,
a thick dewy fog around the city,
and did we really live in four houses in fifteen years,
lose three parents, two cats, a dog, one rabbit,
one goldfish, and three hamsters
but never lost what kept bringing us together
after all that time—the idea that it just didn't
seem right any other way?
Sometimes it seems like a fairy tale,
the way you believed in me
before I believed in myself,
the way your spirit saved me,
the way I still daydream
about the first time I saw you
walking up Olive Street to your cousin's car.

My Father's Son

Here I am,
letting the phone drop on my end
while he slams his into pieces
on the other. We are a thousand miles
apart, acting in unison,
a conversation ending without words.
He does not trust me anymore,
not like the days when I would catch him
after throwing him into the air,
or when he'd lean over the clouds
swirling in my coffee cup, convinced
I could tell him the future.
Now he's sure my predictions
are false and my questions laden
with innuendo. Maybe he's right.

Sometimes it feels like the clock is ticking
when he picks up the phone, the alarm going
off in his head that says, *I have to go,*
and I feel like I am on a game show,
my answer escaping me, drifting out
over the anxious studio audience,
grasping at memory like a tired old man.
I said it would never be this way
but I am my father now,
praying in empty churches,
knees aching,
the clouds gray and hanging over my head.

Always

I was a function-room bartender,
weekends on the beach in the 80's.
It was always the same scene:
young men in ties reaching
for the flying garter belt,
a band with a singer
who had sideburns and a ruffled shirt,
the best man sneaking back from the boys' room
wiping powder off his nose,
the sweet square old ladies
shaking it to the hully gully,
the puffy hair, the tall-neck bottles of beer,
the pink gin fizzes,
and one happy red-faced uncle
setting up the bar again,
Give 'em all one,
and always there was one wild guy
doing a split in the middle of the dance floor,
spilling his drink and bumping
into everyone around him,
and always I'd see him at the end
of the night, his shirttail out,
sweat-stained, smoking a cigarette,
the bride and groom long gone,
the band packed up on the highway home,
the house lights bright.
He'd be talking to a bridesmaid
or somebody's sister about a job he'd lost
or about how he missed his kids
but that he was going to see them soon,
and always this guy would wander over
while I was wiping bottles

or counting the cash drawer.
He'd smile and ask me if I had one on ice,
which I always did, and he'd lay
a ten down on the bar and salute,
like I'd handed him a secret
only the two of us knew.

Justice

for Jack Highberger

We sit in his van, art supplies
and partially scraped palettes
on the floor, my backpack
of poems next to me on the seat.
We drink coffee and tea
looking over the saltwater river
behind Starbucks,
a seagull on a rotted raft,
a sailboat sitting on a mud bank.
He wants to know what's fair
about how America has sold out
to Wall Street and made the middle class
foot the bonus bill. I tell him
nothing is fair, those are the rules.
I tell him I've surrendered.
The problem is too big, I say,
the monster too strong.
I think of it stomping tiny buildings,
villagers running for the hills.

He's not satisfied with my answer
and I know why, the idea
of not setting it right makes no sense to him.
He wants what we all want—justice.
I sip some more tea,
look at the water, the way the dirty
river winds to nowhere,
to the promise of open ocean,
and I think the only way to beat them
is to live in spite of them.

I can help a kid to maybe write
a poem he didn't know he had in him.
He can show that clumsy little girl
how to make a painting
that will change her life.
There's real joy in that, I say.
The other universe operates on its own,
the rich live in a different climate,
all we can do is hope
they don't notice us,
hope they read poetry,
hope they buy art,
hope someday it makes sense to them.

Getting It Right

In grammar school I stuttered,
felt the hot panic on my face
when my turn to read crept up the row.

Even when I counted the paragraphs
and memorized the passage,
I'd trip on the first or second word,

and then it would be over,
the awful hesitation, the word
clinging to the lining of my throat

rising only too late to avoid
the laughter around me. I was never
the smartest kid in the room,

but I had answers I knew were right
yet was afraid to say them.
Years later it all came out, flowing

sentences I practiced over and over,
Shakespeare or Frost, my own tall tales
in low-lit barrooms, scribbled

in black-bound journals, rehearsing,
anticipating my turn, my time,
a way of finally getting it right.

Revere Beach after Hours

It's after midnight, still 90 degrees,
the customers are twenty deep
at each window, most of them drunk,
all of them on the make,
all of them hungry. We push food
at them like one might throw meat
at a wild bear: fried clams,
roast beef sandwiches, lobster rolls.
The more they eat, the more they come,
the line feeding on itself and growing,
like the Blob in the Steve McQueen movie,
or some Trojan war flick
where the soldiers keep coming in waves
no matter how many arrows they take.
The crowd swells after the bars break
and the people are more drunk
with each order and a girl and a guy
make out in the front of the line
and someone yells, *Get a room*,
and a white Cadillac pulls up
to the curb and turns a radio loud.
They all start dancing, long hair,
tight pants, hips moving to the disco beat,
boogie oogie oogie, and a plane
flies low overhead on its way
to East Boston and the sway gets
louder with the laughter and the sidewalk
moves with the motion and the madness
and for a moment I stop what I am doing,
stand with my hands on my hips,
look at the bobbing heads, the hungry mouths,
the dark ocean across the street,
the food hot and waiting behind me.

Looking at an Old Man in the Pleasant Street Tea Room

He holds his hands against his chest.
I just got a haircut, he yells to no one
and no one answers. There are moments
when he smiles, almost chuckles at something
that flashes across his screen.
I know that will be me someday (if I'm lucky)—

What will I remember?
       —a game of spin-the-bottle,
catching frogs with my first dog,
a snow fort as big as a house,
a slow dance in high school,
my dad holding my hand at Fenway Park,
and a man I can't see yelling, *Popcorn.*

My mother remembers things
she can't tell me,
she says, *Did you hear the good news?*
and then grows quiet trying to think of what it was.
The other day she wrapped half a sandwich
in a napkin and asked me
to give it to the man on the television.
She doesn't know it's hard to see her this way.

Is it wrong to want someone to lie down
and go to sleep forever?
I make that wish
with the idea that she'll be with my father again,
the two of them on some tropical island
dancing after dinner, a jazz trio killing it softly.

We all wish for something—the other choice
that Socrates says is not the long dreamless sleep.
Maybe she is already there,
one foot in the water,
connecting to that place
where we can feed our TV heroes
when they are hungry,
that place where everything we remember
is just happening.

Five Days of Rain Dreams

The first dream gave me
                    a week to live. By day four
I was in my backyard

taking buzzer beaters over and over
                    to beat Magic Johnson, then the dream
of my own wake where I stepped out

of the casket and told the crowd
                    at the door to go home, borrowed a pair
of wing-tipped shoes from the undertaker.

The dreams bring the rain in
                    through the slanted windows
like impatient fingers

tapping on the glass
                    bouncing off my forehead in my sleep
like Morse code,

like Chinese torture
                    waking me upright

                    and sweating.

Witness

Maybe it's the first warm
day of spring
and I feel like the world
is waking around me.
Maybe I stop raking
and watch the fat kid on his bike
toss a newspaper to the driveway
and the guy next door waves
to a pickup truck speeding by,
loud rock-and-roll evaporating
down the block,
and maybe I hear a faint scream
from a slightly open window
and garlic cooking somewhere
and tires rolling on
the highway beyond,
one set after another...
and this next part I am certain of:
there's a kid I once knew
bouncing a basketball
on the playground,
he is five feet tall
with an untucked Celtics jersey
over his shorts to his knees,
he is standing at half court
looking toward the tilted half-moon backboard,
yelling over and over again,
Can I get a witness?

Jesus Was a Homeboy

he came with a pillow sack over his shoulder,
took the triple-decker loft that leaked
when it rained, talked all day about the jungle,
the piles of dope, the sins of his M-16,
talked about it when he walked the floor
at three a.m., threw open the window,
and yelled into the street, *Forgiveness,*
talked to the guys on the corner
who bagged his coin and passed him weed
and beat him once good for going on too long,
talked day after day, night after night
talked to the traffic, the cab drivers,
the police, the priests, the nuns,
talked to the guys in the steam room
at the YMCA and the kids playing basketball
in the schoolyard who called him *Jezu the cuckoo.*
Talked in the rectory the night he flipped a table
at a prayer meeting for vets,
walked home with his rosary beads around his fist,
shaved his head, and stood in the rain
in a white satin robe he'd bought overseas,
a few men in a circle around him watching the suffering.

Wishing Well

If wishes were horses, I'd have a ranch.
 —Lucinda Williams

Passing through Ocala, white stucco ranches, orange groves, cypress trees shedding their skin, another line of broken motels stamped with plywood windows, the signs along the road, *large clean rooms, horse country,* we look for gas by a cattle farm, the black and white bellies dotting the hills, the neat rows of thin-roof trailers, the flat brown yards. A church steeple in a field of green points to a cloudless sky and I say to myself, *This is Florida*.

I look in the mirror to catch a glimpse of my teenage kids hooked to iPods in the back seat, and I remember the last time we did this, drove for three days to my mother's, over ten years ago. We took a video of it then but I can't bring myself to look at it. Once in a coffee shop I saw a women look at a child and ask her mother, *Don't you wish you could freeze her?* I've often felt this way, like it's all running away from me too quickly.

I look out the window again, a green pasture, a billboard for fireworks, and a sign advertising a gospel chorus, and a train comes alongside, traveling in the same direction, the same speed, like it caught up to us and slowed down. My wife is sleeping next to me and the kids don't notice that I play this game, beating a series of red lights to keep pace, my nose level with the engine car. It's good luck.

As a boy I walked to Riverside to smoke cigarettes and make wishes when the trains crossed in opposite directions, my grandmother's Irish superstitions still with me, no fake birds hanging on the house, remembering to lift your feet over railroad tracks, tossing pennies into the wishing well.

In those days I was always wishing to start over. It was all very ceremonial and I'd make some promise out loud to God or to the universe, and the wish usually began with an affirmation about beginning again, along with some clever phrase I'd stolen from a Paul Newman movie or a sports magazine, things like *make way for the kid* or *I'm a natural-born world shaker*. I imagined myself doing great things, dangerous things, things people would remember. I had this need to make this day (the one at the time) the day that changed my life. I don't know where that need came from (years later, maybe from mistakes I made), but as a kid, it had to be the Irish in me, the religion. I love the Irish, but we're guilty fuckers.

The sun starts to set and the train switches north away from us, and I imagine he blows his horn three times, and I make a wish that my kids will be safe and protected and, like the Bob Dylan song says, *that [they] see the light surrounding [them]*. Seems I'm still stealing lines for my wishes these days even if I gave up starting over.

The sound of the train wheels on the track is fading, blending with the traffic around me, and I think of the few days before this, fishing behind my mother's condo, throwing back a Sheep Head, and suddenly missing my father sitting on the screen porch.

He kept a small book of prayers he said every night on his knees, hand-scribbled notes about his kids, his wife, casting his net of wishes over all of us, and I'm adding up how many wishes that might be when I turn to see a great blue heron, four feet away, looking for a piece of shrimp I'd already thrown into the ocean.

I'm sorry, I say, just like that, out loud, and I tuck my line to my pole and we walk off the pier together.

Here on the west coast, looking out at the Tampa Bay Bridge, I will always feel the same sadness, the same longing to have done things a little differently in my youth, to have been less impetuous, perhaps, less self-destructive. I remember when my kids were little, two and four, maybe, I said to my father in the house I grew up in, *I'm sorry for those years it was so crazy. It must have been hard.* He just looked at me, a note of confirmation, not entirely releasing me, not willingly wanting to remember it either. It was a silent moment.

The train has just about disappeared on its way to Bradenton or points north and it feels like an ending to a movie, the credits of my life rolling slowly over the screen, Lucinda Williams singing some soulful ballad as we all fade to black. One of the kids asks to stop for a bathroom, but I'm not really listening. I'm still back there with my father's prayers sprinkled over the backwater he loved so much, standing among the herons and the pelicans and the catfish, waiting over all that blue for a wish or two of my own.

Not Much to It

You draw with chalk
on your sidewalk.
You ride your bike.
You go for ice cream
with your friends.
You party in college.
You get to figuring
by the fire
on a cold night
in the mountains.
You listen to jazz
on the ocean.
You catch a ball game
now and then.
You cradle with
different folks till you
find one who fits.
Then you wake up one day
sitting on a creaky porch
missing your kids,
patting your dog,
drinking a can of cold beer,
the summer like a blanket
on your shoulders,
and something you knew
floats by in the night sky
just out of reach.

Things I've Lost

My father's wedding ring
my tax returns
my bronze baby shoes
my orange high-cut sneakers
my first Christmas ornament
my innocence
my ability to play defense
on a basketball court
some of my friends (living and dead)
some of the wonder
some of the grace
some of the time I spent
looking for love
or God
or something to fix me

that one week when I was twenty six
all of it lost somewhere,
that sick feeling in my gut
running to New York, for what?
That was the day I lost a big
chunk of it, the gray two-families
out the train window staring back at me
like the sentries of some ancient prison,
and I'm reaching out with both hands
trying to pull the day back from where it came.

From Another Day

I play a Tony Bennett CD
I bought for her birthday.
Ninety years old this May.
She is reading the paper
beneath the arched glass atrium
stained with pollen and inchworms.
It's a sunny morning, a slight breeze
from the beach a few hundred yards away,
and I look at her, her foot
tapping slightly, her gaze far away,
as if she has already crossed over.
She blinks and her eyes fill.
Are you okay? I ask
and make a joke about choosing
different music next time.
I give her some water and a tissue.
So many memories, she says
and I put my arm around her
thin shoulder. *We all meet up again
someday,* I tell her and instantly
I feel a heavy lump of shame
in my throat, like I've given
her directions I'm not sure of,
a second-hand story disguised as the truth.

Poetry Snob

I listen to a young poet from Maine at the Mass
Poetry Festival. She reads a poem about sentences,
appropriate language, quoting grammar rules and
Wikipedia. She's smart and it's clever
and she reads it with big flip cards that she says
can be used in any order. But it's long
and after seven flip cards I can't fight
that feeling in my gut that has me wishing
for a tree limb and a rope. I know I'm my own brand
of poetry snob, and the little voice in my head
tells me I'm no better than Vonnegut (his insistence
on rhyme)—*no fair tennis without a net.*
But actually it's not rhyme I'm missing, it's story.
And just then I look out the window next
to the young poet from Maine and I see what could be
a mother and a daughter arguing, a baby in a stroller
between them. The mother is smoking a cigarette
and she looks like life has gotten the best of her,
and the daughter, a chip off the old block, yells
something back, and they ping-pong insults
until they both turn away and get quiet
like all's been said that needs to be said.
Then they each grab a piece of the stroller and walk out
of the frame, and I roll-focus to the Maine poet
still flipping her cards, and part of me wants to stand up
and confess my snobbery, while the rest of me wishes
she would read something human, something dangerous.
Forget the net, I want to yell, *swing for the fence.*

The Same Old Story

Living the white-shirt life
rolled to the elbows
people leaving dollars
cold beer whiskey
cigarette smoke, and juke-box music
a Hank Williams song
bouncing off the walls
the same stories
from the night before
that's a funny one, Joe
sprinkle the infield
sprinkle the outfield

each night
the same no-tell basement hideaway
the same husbands dodging their wives
the same guy selling drugs
to a guy selling cars
the same drama
tell the bitch I'm not here
the same movie
flipping by me like a Kinetograph
like a recurring dream
like a bad habit
like the highway to Florida,
one sign after another
Stuckey's, Stuckey's, Stuckey's.

Siberian Dwarfs

At first we bought a pair, a glass tank, and what looked like
a tiny Ferris wheel. They seemed happy; the wheel spinning
all day and night, squeaking like the hum of exercise equipment
in the gym. They even took turns on it. Then it happened,
number one *over-exercised*, the guy at the pet store told us,
a heart attack or a stroke, so I moved number two
to the kitchen counter from my daughter's bedroom,
gave him something to look at since his workout partner had died,
but that was the sunny side of the house and the glass tank
got too warm, way too warm, like a sauna, and heat stroke
did him in, so we bought number three who must have heard
about the others 'cause he spent all day standing on the top
of the Ferris wheel trying to jump out of the tank. I felt bad
he was so neurotic. I carried him around the house in my pocket,
his little gray head peeking out, biting my finger when I went
to pick him up. He lived almost three weeks that way,
taking daily rides like a kangaroo cub, till I found him dead one morning,
buried beneath the shavings, stretched out on his side, tiny pink eyes
shut tight, almost like he was satisfied to have lived so long,
or maybe he was just happy not to be hitching a ride
in someone's lint-caked pocket, or baking in the sun, or chasing himself
on a squeaky wheel run that had no end.

Bob's Story

for Bob Evans

It was not my first funeral.
That was my godmother,
the funeral putty stuck on her nose
so I wanted to pick it,
but this one, this was Glen,
my dad's nephew and drinking buddy,
the reason for my middle name.

Glen came and went once before I was born
to escape his alcoholic mother,
then came back when I was twelve
to die the death of a drunk—
a handful of pills and a bottle of booze.

I was with my dad the night he heard,
backing the Belvedere into the driveway
the way he always did,
then breaking down in front of me.
I remember putting an arm around him,
like a scene from a movie,
the two of us in the glare from the dashboard
of the '65 Plymouth.

Get Thee to a Nunnery

I drive five hours to a convent in New Jersey
where a nun tells us about her disabled pets
and the smoke alarm and how the doors will close
electronically if there's too many crumbs in the toaster
and she reminds us to bring our cell phones
if we go walking in the woods because one retreatist
got stuck in the mud and had to call for help,
and we write poems all weekend from prompts,
poems about our children, our husbands, our wives,
our dreams, our fears, and I realize, sitting at a wooden table
under a statue of Saint Joseph (someone said he looks like Tolstoy),
that I don't have a poem about my penis like some
other folks had the night before, or a poem about
anyone else's penis for that matter, and suddenly
I feel inadequate.

Later that night I sleep in Saint Bridgette's Room
(we all have saints above our doors)
with a hooded sweatshirt on like I'm camping
in the White Mountains, and the radiator outside
my door is silent and staring at me like some quiet kid
I knew in grade school, and I dream, in between shivering,
of an undefeated seventh-grade basketball team,
and in the morning I look out the window at the snow
expecting a deer to peek out from the forest
and I think, *Get thee to a nunnery*
if you want to write a poem worth anything.

At the Car Hop, 2015

after Bukowski

I'm parked in my car, the windows down,
waiting for a cheeseburger at Scotty Dog
on the corner of Rantoul and Elliot.
The light Sunday traffic cruises by,
one or two cars pull into the lined spaces
around me. I watch a bearded man
with a fishing pole at a picnic table
under an umbrella. He plays a Journey song
loud on his radio, *I'm forever yours…faithfully*.
He drums along to it, his hands moving in time
next to his shopping cart:
a few plastic bags draped on the handles,
bottles and cans stacked in the belly.
The girl who comes to the car window for my order
has one dark tooth and tattooed legs.
I ask her for salt and she brings me a small plastic cup of it.
The air is heavy and I could be sad if I thought about it
but just like that I'm in no hurry to go anywhere.
I don't care how long it takes to make my burger, my fries.
I just want to listen to the song, hang my arm out the window,
feel the waves of summer heat off the street,
and sip from my cool bottle of Ipswich root beer.

Coffee Shop

So I wander into this coffee shop
after class one day and some Russian guy
serves me tea in a pot and a coffee-
cake muffin and I start to work on the crime novel
I'm writing when I'm not teaching
and this middle-aged brunette woman
sits in the opposite corner by herself
and then a bald guy in a shirt and tie
comes to meet her and they start talking
about *the court case* and I realize
this guy's the fuzz and then right
on his tail comes this older guy with
gray hair and a striped shirt
and a bottle blonde on his arm and I look
at his nose, wrapped in a bandage
that covers half of his face, and I think
of Jack Nicholson in *Chinatown,* and a young girl
sits at a table nearby typing with her back to me,
her hair tied tight in a bun, some half-eaten
sandwich on her plate and the Russian guy
says something to someone I can't see
in a quick burst of broken English
and the cop gets louder with each new piece
to his story and the guy with the nose
looks at me like I'm staring too long,
and out of nowhere a woman with a camera
snaps a picture and just like that my coffee
is cold and any minute I'm expecting
someone to yell, *Cut,* and lower the dolly
from the ceiling and the whole place lights a cigarette.

Motion Picture Family

The first time was wide-screen Cinerama,
soldiers with arrow-pierced chests,
war-painted Indians, a thunderous posse racing
over my head, the blazing desert sun.
I think I fell asleep by the end, but I remember
rifle blasts, the dirt- and blood-flecked faces of the cavalry,
the bottomless bowl of buttered popcorn,
the warm stale cola, the dust-speckled
purr of the projector.

Not long after, I chased the reruns on my own:
Bogart and Dooley Wilson in French-occupied Morocco,
the letters of transit and the black-market cafés,
the slapstick streams of Keystone Kops flailing after
a fire engine,
and Chaplin, my hero, managing his way
around the brutes and the thieves
with an acrobatic dance and a sly grin.

I grew up with the movies always on my mind,
pretending scenes in my backyard,
taking a bullet to the ground like Cagney,
staring myself down in the mirror
and swigging water like John Wayne's whiskey,
running like Jim Brown with an arm
full of hand grenades.

My movie world was safe, the bad guys lost,
the bullies couldn't get me,
the scared little kid was a gun-toting cowboy,
a tough guy, a wizard, a hero.

When my own children were young, they made
Barbie movies—sitting her in a car and turning on
the fan so the blonde hair blew behind her
on an imaginary mountain road. My son,
the Hi-8 cameraman, my daughter the set designer.
We had no TV in those days so I'd bring home
a monitor and a VCR from work and we'd rent
Goonies, The Princess Bride, The Parent Trap.
We rated them, watched them over
and over to decide if we liked them, stayed curled up
in blankets, drunk with hot chocolate.

They laughed at me, even then, if I cried,
which I always did when the music rose in waves
and I fell again for the Hollywood touch,
however predictable or corny.

Once when they were eight and ten, my wife and I
drove them in a blizzard to Hollywood Hits
to see a romantic comedy. We kept saying,
This is crazy, as we plowed through the snow,
laughing later in the empty theater.

We chased this motion picture love affair
to the Kendall Square Cinema in Cambridge,
our favorite haunt, paid attention to the listings,
drove forty minutes to see two (and one time three)
movies in the same day—French action films,
Korean monster movies, dark and gritty reels of noir.

Still today my daughter calls to tell me
she scored tickets for a premiere at the Brattle
and my son sends a text to say he's seen
a Paul Thomas Anderson movie four times.

We are a family who needs our films,
making movies ourselves, reading and writing scripts,
always playing the critic. Always being fans. We love
picking winners for the Academy Awards, we love watching
the films we love again and again, the ninety-plus minutes
of life-affirming action, the small stories on the big screen.
We love being frightened or made sad. We love rooting
for unlikely heroes. We love munching popcorn in the dark
with a hundred strangers and staying in our seats
until the credits have rolled and the kids in the aisles
are working the brooms.

Heaven

A middle-aged woman in a gray pantsuit let me in through a stone gate with roses climbing over the top of a trellis. *You'll love it here,* she said. *It's always sunny and 70.* The grass was green and the trees were turning fall colors and the ocean spread out on both sides of me as far as I could see, white-capped waves exploding against a rocky shore. A few wispy clouds hung in a blue sky. I walked into a park with a neat trimmed lawn where a picnic was in full swing, lots of folks playing guitars in front of crossed-legged hippies, singing folk songs or ballads with words like *fella* and *train whistle.* I saw groups of teens in jeans playing catch with a football, a few throwing Frisbees. There were no cars in sight but I did smell marijuana. A guy with black-framed glasses poured me a cup of tea from a pewter pot. He offered me cookies and sliced strawberries on a small white dish as he added cream to my cup. *Just the way you like it,* he said. I spent most of the afternoon chatting with folks I didn't know, small talk about the earth and being human. At one point we played basketball, four on four, and I hit every shot I took but no one seemed to notice. There were small square pizza slices and cold beer for lunch and everyone in the park had a dog doing tricks, jumping through hoops, rolling over, playing dead. I took a nap in the afternoon under a willow tree, listening to someone reading a story by James Baldwin. When I opened my eyes they were all gone. It was just me, the sun setting over the ocean, a cool breeze on my face, and everywhere I looked there were baby rabbits jumping.

Death Wish

I want to be able to fly
like I did in the dreams I had,
three feet off the ground
and up the sides of buildings.

I want to be able to see live history:
the Civil War
from a lawn chair at Gettysburg,
dine in outer space when they
hit a golf ball on the moon.

I want it to be special, magical,
worth the wait,
after being afraid for so long.

Waiting

In the dream I am as tall as you (six foot two).
We are playing basketball in the gym,

the two of us pulling up for jump shots.
I am as good as you too, just as quick

and no one wins, no one misses.
We sweat and squeak our sneakers

trying to guard each other
and when it's over we shake hands,

towels draped around our necks,
and walk out to the empty campus,

the leaves covering the ground,
the chapel and the brick buildings dark,

the air cool, the sun setting
behind the Worcester hills when we walk past

the duck pond and the library
and onto Salisbury Street.

Remember that time, you say, and we laugh
as you move away on the sidewalk

and the dusk overtakes you,
but I keep standing long after you're gone,

the empty darkness around me
waiting for the sun to come up.

Reading to My Kids

When they were little I read
to them at night until my tongue
got tired. They would poke me
when I started to nod off after twenty pages
of Harry Potter or Lemony Snicket.
I read (to them) to get them to love reading
but I was never sure if it was working
or if it was just what I was supposed to do.
But one day, my daughter (fifteen then)
was finishing *Of Mice and Men* in the car
on our way to basketball.
She was at the end when I heard her say,
No, in a familiar frightened voice
and I knew right away where she was.
"Let's do it now," Lennie begged,
"Let's get that place now."
"Sure, right now. I gotta. We gotta,"
and she started crying, then I started crying,
and I think I saw Steinbeck
in the back seat nodding his head,
and it felt right to me,
like I'd done something right,
and I thought to myself, *Keep going,*
read it to me, please, please, I can take it.

ACKNOWLEDGMENTS

These poems were published, some in slightly different form, in the following journals:

Chagrin River Review: "Chicago," "Wishing Well"
Comstock Review: "Jesus Was a Homeboy"
Getting Old: "Looking at an Old Man in the Pleasant Street Tea Room"
Gival Press/ArLiJo: " Get Thee to a Nunnery"
Hamilton Stone Review: "From Another Day"
Juked: "Justice"
Like One: "Revere Beach after Hours"
New Writing: "Creative Writing at Osgood Park, Salem, September 7, 2010"
Paddlefish: "Newburyport," "Summer Storms"
Paterson Literary Review: "At the Car Hop, 2015," "Fairy Tale," "Getting It
    Right," "A Holiday Poem," "My Father's Son," "Poetry Snob"
Review Americana: "Home Movie"
Salem Writers: "A Surreal Poem"
South 85: "Witness"
Zig Zag Folios: "Bob's Story," "Five Days of Rain Dreams," "Siberian Dwarfs"

I'd like to thank the Salem Writers for critiquing so many of these poems and for their continued inspiration, especially J. D. Scrimgeour, January Gill O'Neil, Cindy Veach Lappetito, Dawn Paul, Lis Weiss Horowitz, Joe McGurn, Jennifer Colella Martelli, Jim DeFilippi, Danielle Jones-Pruett, Colleen Michaels, Clay Ventre, and M. P. Carver. I'm grateful also to the New Jersey poets who have helped me so much over the years: Mark Hillringhouse, R. G. Evans, and Laura Boss. A special thanks to Maria Mazziotti Gillan, Afaa Michael Weaver, Starr Troup, Baron Wormser, Dawn Potter, and Joan Cusack Handler. I'd also like to thank my kids, Kevin and Michaela, and my wife, Betty, for sharing their lives with me. Finally, I thank my friends Ed, Jack, and Tim for always being a phone call away.

CAVANKERRY'S MISSION

CavanKerry Press is committed to expanding the reach of poetry to a general readership by publishing poets whose works explore the emotional and psychological landscapes of everyday life.

OTHER BOOKS IN THE
EMERGING VOICES SERIES

Jesus Was a Homeboy, Kevin Carey
Eating Moors and Christians, Sandra M. Castillo
Esther, Pam Bernard
Love's Labors, Brent Newsom
Places I Was Dreaming, Loren Graham
Misery Islands, January Gill O'Neil
Spooky Action at a Distance, Howard Levy
door of thin skins, Shira Dentz
Where the Dead Are, Wanda S. Praisner
Darkening the Grass, Michael Miller
The One Fifteen to Penn Station, Kevin Carey
My Painted Warriors, Peggy Penn
Neighborhood Register, Marcus Jackson
Night Sessions, David S. Cho
Underlife, January Gill O'Neil
The Second Night of the Spirit, Bhisham Bherwani
Red Canoe: Love in Its Making, Joan Cusack Handler
WE AREN'T WHO WE ARE and this world isn't either, Christine Korfhage
Imago, Joseph O. Legaspi
Through a Gate of Trees, Susan Jackson
Against Which, Ross Gay
The Silence of Men, Richard Jeffrey Newman
The Disheveled Bed, Andrea Carter Brown
The Fork Without Hunger, Laurie Lamon
The Singers I Prefer, Christian Barter
Momentum, Catherine Doty
An Imperfect Lover, Georgianna Orsini
Soft Box, Celia Bland
Rattle, Eloise Bruce
Eye Level: Fifty Histories, Christopher Matthews
GlOrious, Joan Cusack Handler
The Palace of Ashes, Sherry Fairchok
Silk Elegy, Sondra Gash
So Close, Peggy Penn
Kazimierz Square, Karen Chase
A Day This Lit, Howard Levy

Printing this book on 30-percent PCW and FSC certified paper saved 2 trees, 1 million BTUs of energy, 127 pounds of CO_2, 67 pounds of solid waste, and 524 gallons of water.